House of McQueen

House of McQueen

Valerie Wallace

Four Way Books

Tribeca

Excerpt from "Late Apollo" from THE REST OF LOVE by Carl Phillips. Copyright © 2004 by Carl Phillips. Reprinted by permission of Farrar, Straus and Giroux.

Library of Congress Cataloging-in-Publication Data

Names: Wallace, Valerie, 1968- author.
Title: House of McQueen / Valerie Wallace.
Description: New York, NY : Four Way Books, [2018] | Includes bibliographical references.
Identifiers: LCCN 2017029369 | ISBN 9781945588112 (pbk. : alk. paper)
Classification: LCC PS3623.A359836 A6 2018 | DDC 811/.6--dc23
LC record available at https://lccn.loc.gov/2017029369

This book is manufactured in the United States of America and printed on acid-free paper.

Funding for this book was provided in part by a generous donation in memory of John J. Wilson.

Four Way Books is a not-for-profit literary press. We are grateful for the assistance we receive from individual donors, public arts agencies, and private foundations.

PROUD MEMBER

We are a proud member of the Community of Literary Magazines and Presses.

Distributed by University Press of New England
One Court Street, Lebanon, NH 03766

In the depths of our darkness . . . the whole place is for Beauty.

—Rene Char

It wasn't really about fashion, with Lee. It was so much more than that.
It was about everything that was to do with being alive.

—Sarah Burton

For Marc

Contents

Council House, 1972   3

Fabrication   4

[When staggering down the runway wearing tartan over torn lace]   5

Shears   6

Bumsters   7

Needles   8

Let's make a dress from these   9

The Young Ornithologists Club, 1979   10

McQueen Linen   11

& for a moment they   12

I like a good Grimm tale   13

McQueen Self-Portrait as Bestiary   14

Small seams   19

Savile Row, 1985   20

Bespoke   22

Central St. Martins College of Art and Design, 1991   29

From the Shoulder   31

Haute Couture (acrostic)   32

Studded   33

McQueen Tartan   34

McQueen's Bop with the Interviewer   35

Secrets & Fabulations   37

Whisper the Water   39

Dub Bill / Double Stich   42

Obsession Dream 43

Charm for Protection 44

I Dance Like Flames 45

I'm a Free Bitch 46

In this one there are dancers 47

Dream of Nature 48

McQueen Neoprene 49

[I knew a woman when I saw one, though] 51

McQueen Cashmere 52

House of McQueen 53

Winged 54

Silhouette for the 21st Century 56

Autobiography of Alexander McQueen 57

But There on the Shining 59

Joyce & Lee 63

Lee 64

Notes

Council House, 1972

When I was about 3 years old, I drew a dress on the wall. And what dress was it? *Cinderella.*

When she turned, I'd never seen anything like it.
Dress made for charming prince and fairy.
I could manage the little sleeves, tiny waist rising
Out of skirts which laughed as they traveled with her across the ballroom floor.
And they had stars woven in them.
I got caught wondering, how to draw that color—sea coast changing to dawn.
There was trouble, but I didn't care. I knew it was the dress
That saved her. All the rest was just a story.

Fabrication

I don't understand my own mind,
Though I use my own dream. I've just eaten
An orange and put the peel to dry
On top of the stove so I can smell it.
It would be very rash to say
A brilliant cross-light does comprehend
The unrelenting world. I'm still waiting
For my soul to catch up with me. I can
Take people in ones and twos but at dinner
Everyone's full of shit. Some are bad
With a bit of good in them and some
Are good with a bit of bad in them. In the last
Light of evening, chance to look through endless corridors.
As it flapped off—see? The world is not a mirror.

[When staggering down the runway wearing tartan over torn lace]

When staggering down the runway wearing tartan over torn lace

When thin leather sheaths ripped across the chest

When hooded silk robes fallen open

When bodies a ravaged country

When inner thighs smudged with red

When only gored grey lace covers the body

When breasts exposed from an unbloused jacket

When stocks edged with a Stuart ruff enclose the neck

When obsolete colors, fulwe, sad, vernal, watchet

When sleeveless torn satin & cutaway shorts

When strewn with cigarette butts

When a buried history of England & Scotland

When a man yelling, Have I offended you then?

When the body becomes everything it is given

Shears

Silk tweed gray felt sable damask flannel
Glory of a sharp tool be the lasting part of me

Plip scut slew slew all sounds fall still
Have you seen the fox? Which way did he

Go, he go? Hither and thither clean sheets
Somersault boundary for a thimble's jig

Double-tonguing a syncopated flute
Listen sharply: the hues are parting

Sliding up and from the blazing center
No slake for hunger   Of quick, of nimble

Two ships run together like quicksilver
Driven by a storm along the littoral

I've cut away the waste. Curved flay of shears.
It's only cloth, whisper scissors in my ears.

Bumsters

I cut
a path to
the sacred
tired of
suggestion
I turned her
to the side
plumbed
the plum
cupped
her saucer
lowered
the drape
to her small
place
of want
at the back
eye touch
where she
pleases I
dropped
something
I found
something

Needles

When we love at night and I don't know
The people who will feed me & the moon
Turns blue. Maybe extra licentiousness, or
Affectionate games, maybe body's true
Beauty & its soothing filth. When the world
Strips down, love is first a lesson
& then like a mattress's teeth, steps into the mirror.
When I stare & brood as I do often
On manliness of all brutal acts, we
Fetch each other in and out of shadows. Our
Wrestle with hair, what dress to wear. Needles
Of down, parachutes of arrested color
Tied with fangs. I may be tough & selfish but what
Do you expect? I think with my bare hands.

Let's make a dress from these

Stained red medical slides layer vertically on sleeveless sheath,
high-necked and cut away from right shoulder to right hipbone.
Heavy overskirt of crimson ostrich feathers swish & switch,
thick & deliberate into plum-black feathered underskirt. They
obey the law of push. From the slightest pressure, they bloom.

    Interpreter of alarm
    Lover of syringe & tub water
    Tongue at your throat
    One thousand thin clappers
    Summon the carnal bell
    Raucous rouge
    Smudge of poppies
    Murder of corpuscular roses
    So juiced they vogue
    Rubies strewn on scarlet carpet
    You stare. There is fire racing
    Under your skin.
    Twin to eros
    Close your eyes to see me
    Repeat me to feel me
    At the end I go quietly
    I take you with me.

The Young Ornithologists Club, 1979

Here it has facts about birds.

Did you know when a peregrine falcon flies, it is the fastest animal?

Here's where I copied a barn owl. I call him Barmy Barny! He has a
   mask for a face.

This is where you write the birds you've seen.

I've got swift, rook, ring dove pigeon, wryneck, house sparrow, house
   martin, red-backed shrike.

That's a pipit. That's my drawing of a flock of skylarks.

That one was a dead pigeon. Haha! Poor thing. But they're lovely
   things, really.

Mostly I come up here to watch them fly. After school, before night,

They're a sight when they swoop and turn, or late day sit and preen
   away

Like their life depended on it. When I'm up here I'm myself,

I can hold an idea in my mind. Music as well, sometimes. Your mind
   rides a current

With them. Look at that one, coming this way—

McQueen Linen

I design the shows   as stills   if you look they tell   the whole story

when I find   I've   no place for fear   I show myself

the body's   tried to tell you   it's intricate   altered

perimeter   what I see   our bodies'   silver / dream

I will not   gesture   wreckage   but radiant / waking

pull back   toward   the way we   all of us, born

if you take   everything, you   have got   to let everything go

even my / skull   will soon be   uncovered   / still

& for a moment they

Pre-war muslin blushes over dusk silk,
Hidden silver carriage encages sternum to mons,
Bodice & skirt, color of milky tea spilled
Onto Ceylon plantation parchment, into hourglass outline

Whose arms are a girl's which flow in a movement
The foreigner thinks indecent, zarabande.
He sips, & ships. Handel slows it to a drawing room vibrato
In plain sight of stays & crushed blossoms.

Funnel neck filled with chrysanthemums, peonies, allium,
From the sleeves, too, they tumble & decay
Out of the earth's trench, & for a moment
They lift their unmasked lavish faces.

I like a good Grimm tale

I was the highwayman riding hard through inky nights, for the one gone mad with longing. The devoted who prepared your bed for sleep. Skirt of jet beads scallop-stitched over silk, and under, silk rustles against my boot.

Damascene like waters of a tarn, wide embroidered panels of leaves sewn thickly, and from each shoulder, soft suggestion of forest floor. Sleeves accept outsized cuffs of pleats, bound at the wrists as if by an embouchure.

When I enter the room, claret is paused before parted lips, wrought iron lamp surrenders its spill. I need no bell, no whip, no horse's tail. I am your black tulip in the garden. Dark soul, only one of us sure of this world.

McQueen Self-Portrait as Bestiary

i.   *Raven*

Fill myself with chthonic things,

Always close to the underworld but not of it

Too busy stealing & yanking information from every direction.

Tick my satisfaction by seconds.

Know the difference between raven & crow?   Histrionics.

My mind jabs, tilts.

I love a clean line.

Look at these bones, foil, bits of fur—

I'll use my own feathers if I have to,

You hear me? You hear me? You hear me? You hear me?

ii.   *Snake*

My ears are filled with all this sky.

I make my way through your orchard, find the fallen, fermented, honor their use for my use.

Every skin I leave behind, a flamboyance, a chronicle. Each of them, a yes. Yes.

iii. Moth

I memory the cloud

My mother spun

Around me

Dirt birthed me

My soul thrusts in & out

With all this rustling

Every night I must

Get hold of some brilliance

iv.   *Jellyfish*

The moon whispers like a sting in the sea.

Feels like millions of years I've gathered and worried the thick current.

Armorless, I am threaded with blades. The moon turns blue,

Murmurs *No heart, no heart.* I am a festival of longing.

v.   *Hawk*

Constellation skimming the unknown world,

My velocity a kind of screed.

When from my highest perch I keen the mouse's movement

And the mouse who turns to peer up, sees only sun

I am the angel, and the demon

When I finish into him.

Which is all I want, to use the bright,

To make quick destruction. To dive to it.

Small seams

Beauty is an accusation. Nature
Herself has turned metaphysical.
Skull bears witness, proper
& perfect. Viper to socket, startles
me into alertness. Profane
& beauty are not in opposition —
Mediocrity is the world's welter. Flame
On the altar, from dulled procession
The age demanded an image of its
Accelerated grimace. I'd be a fool
Not to open my mind. Don't pity
The age if I mirror it. I want to pull
Nature into vanity. To lead back.
Let the skull crack. Let the wind speak.

Savile Row, 1985

I am a cunt

I may have scrawled with chalk on the interlining

Of one of the coats I cut for that royal tab
Whose job it is to sit on his arse

All day and get paid for it. Only O'Calloghan
Has my polite side; at 16,

I work as hard as any of them. Learned
To not bite the thread, hold shears properly.

Fail, hope, fail, hope. Thimble on middle finger
How I push through canvas, horsehair, velvet.

Dress coats, morning coats, jackets, trousers.
At 17 I cut for perfection.

Measure by instinct—rock of eye, is how we
Say it. My button holes, immaculate.

Wool of untroubled sheep, drafted, cut, bundled.
Not that I need talk of the world's grimness

Constantly, but some awareness would be
Nice. None of them here ever stole his sister's

Bra off the clothesline and wore it screaming
Down the streets! No one ever paid for it

Like I did. I sewed my sisters' dresses
When I was 10 cos we could not afford

To buy them. There's work and there's work. When they
Caught me they pulled me down. A good story now.

I had rather fight and scream than hide
Under my mother's bed. God, I'm hungry lately.

Bespoke

1. Made out of Naomi Campbell's words.

Who was I—asking with women and concepts
The whole butterfly night of the world and why
A wing in a mirror could interpret
It, and the body's grief and courage. My
Life begins with every question I face,
In each wild shape my surgery finds
When I call out my name with my touch.
I know the deep privacy of the possibly lost.
Am I meant to be tempted as I am,
Unwrap intimacy, take its top off,
Go deeper, to nerve and blood and calm.
Everything feels wild. Nothing feels young.
I have found beauty, pulled back the cover,
And in my time was some kind of wonder.

2. *Made out of Kate Moss' words.*

When I started out, fashion aspired to trends.
Designers still traffic together,
Obviously. Now I've got lots of friends
Still I show both sides: beautiful and vulgar.
I don't see myself as what people buy.
Sleeve, skirt, legs, hips, wedding, glamour: perfect
Fit. I never rest til the details get right.
Know what I mean? Exposed defect.
Nasty is gorgeous when you work it.
Find your art in each element. Nothing is precious
In my house. Nightmares paired with red tartan,
Frocks undone by marvelous vices.
Perform my clothes like you're devastated.
I'm not finished 'til you're implicated.

3. *Made out of Helena Bonham Carter's words.*

God knows I've got a healthy bit of self-loathing
But I'm the sort of person to get on with it.
Work clears out the drama. I don't actually like fighting.
I take pleasure in discipline. It's what made me — that,
And not being concerned with how others perceive me.
I'm not about to exploit suffering in my shows
But I make a choice to see the damaged and bizarre.
Monstrous and magical are roots of the same emotion. How
To invent the narrative cupboard, to be honest beyond costume?
I tangle Victorian with tulle, fancy with natural.
Sometimes black and white, sometimes tangerine. There's room
In fashion to give yourself up, isn't there, to a kind of proposal
Of intuition. This is what is more and more with me.
I wasn't ready before, to obey strange dreams I couldn't see.

4. *Made out of Isabella Blow's words.*

For instance, today I slashed fragility.
I'm not a nun in a bloody convent.
I haven't got a fashion personality.
I snort. I'm a pig, not a silent
Flower. Nothing happens by being mute.
My hands, my mouth, explore borders
To close the body. Even suicide
Has a cloth. I design armor for
The battlefield. I cast power into
The subjective, show hideous as delicious.
Look at the ostrich who clomps in duck shoes.
The tuna who desires more than deep sea hush.
Does my craftsmanship exact a price? Darling, come.
One thing's for certain. We'll never die of boredom.

5. *Made out of Björk's words.*

I nourish the urges we're born with,

Not to be outrageous [laughs], but to listen

To hunger, the will to prowl. Life's organic clash,

That's the current I skim for each collection.

I'm not interested in emotionally restrictive *outfits.*

When I use a cage, it's so people can see the danger

Of tyranny, like racism, or when nationhood spits

Religion. I want to push people so they stop

Walking past what they feel. Yes, design is manipulation.

Building a new angle, attempting opposite of what was thought

Style could do. Each show full volume, no restriction;

This is how I put an idea in people's minds.

People will remember integrity, won't they?

Sometimes I feel such urgency—

6. *Made out of Amy Mullins' words.*

The runway's terrain is my church.
I want people to shout, whipped good, a place
Where claws & glory ignite the soul.
We neglect beauty unless we make space
To display our frightened & deficient.
Magnolias & grapevines wait
To be stepped into. Ours is the ancient
Shadow of constant existence, weighted
With generations which tell us to hide.
If I have learned how to claim my own
Decrepit existence with clean lines
& the double realm of abandon
It is because you have watched me do it—
You who were made different, through it.

7. Made out of Annabelle Nielson's words.

I never thought it was a coincidence, that I loved water.
More than whispering stars, a sort of protective,
Surrounding peace. Ocean darkness has that power.
I may not be especially religious, but a choice to believe
Anything but wonder is taken from you when you dive. Mutely,
I find inspiration at the bottom of the sea.
Midnight, moonlight, excitement, flare: beauty
Living by its own private energy. Nothing about the ocean is weak.
It's got its own vocabulary; it's millions of one true moment.
The ocean gives & what it gave me is I felt understood,
Found closure & renewed vision in a place so vibrant.
A bit like singing inside a gospel choir: for a time you could
Believe you were a vessel—but if you kept at it, you'd
Discover you were just a gold thread weaving through.

Central St. Martins College of Art
and Design, 1991

She stares at me like I'm trying to sell her something. I haven't got
much time, she says, and lifts a dress from the pile I threw on her
couch. Gigli's pattern? she asks, turning it over, and then, You
were in Milan? Your pattern? I nod each time and she lifts them
all. God, I know I'm fatter than anyone here. I could do this job.
Outside, little groups of students clutch their cigarettes. Inside,
scent of so much fabric, sewing machine grease, air clean as a lemon.
Her desk piled with books bright as exotic birds.

She's got a hum. She draws her breath in, looks at me. Can you
draw, she says. I have my O-levels in art, I say. They made me draw. . .
fruit. She smiles at that. That night, I dream about him who tried
to hollow me out when I was six years old to eleven. I wake up in
sweat like I'm back at my first job, washing up in the bar where a
man would get glassed for looking wrong. Five days ago I was cutting
Gigli's patterns and arguing in a language I don't speak on his factory
floor. How easy it is now, ripping out and starting again.

I come back 3 days later with my sketches, but can't look away from
those wankers and their shiny portfolios. I very much doubt they
know proportion, dimension. What are they, 2 years younger, she
says. You couldn't be their teacher. My face gets hot as a bruise. We
have a Master's Course, though scholarships have been taken, she
says, But I would like to make a place for you here. She uses the word

difficult in a sentence, which makes us both laugh. A small worry of money is about to spill in my brain, but I hold it away. The room of her voice might be a pattern, too.

From the Shoulder

Impala antlers ratchet

Small details of air

2 glazed coils strike the sky

My crescent scars ripple

Improbably soft pony pelt

My pronk, my strot, my

Sewing needle walk

~~Fragile fragile~~

Nimble   careful

My gaze a slow burn,

Shawl lapel, single breasted

This / I want

I won't be caught

Whither of quiver

Fits my waist

Extends like a hand

Down to the hinge

Where leg

Where hip

The lift that says

Come

      hither

Haute Couture (acrostic)

At the first, a promise to share the fireflies in your brain with

the crickets in my brain, gift the heart-shaped apricot at my

end for your bunspark unpuckered, your stalk of young maple in the gorge

of the river you brought with you. Reach your hand in this fashion.

The discovery of how to really bite dark cherries. Swollen bordercall into me into yourself

day in day out. Arm :: swan :: fumble :: ruddle :: winker :: fist :: throttle into the unforgiving current gathering stones.

They're spun from their beds and they are comprehended. I know you are

only, no matter how we relish this thing we do. Look at us, our radiant cooling. Relinquish your

clothes. I'll cut you mine.

Studded

An aurora borealis of raindrops. How striking
They will look on the bodice of her dance frock—
Diamond dusted with rain drop fragments. A kissing
Like the sea opened its lips, smelling of
A whore's dream. Salt perfume of the sea anodyne
Of the lonely. Laughing and leaning back
To lie there, watching it, like someone diving.
Night passes in black chiffon. Last night I woke
Up laughing, the dram shop in the dream shop.
Suppose you had your life to live over.
Wind riffing water fingering spruce.
It was funny, having no money of my own.
Rain in rain circles. Needle like my lover.
I can't get over how it all works in together.

McQueen Tartan

there is   blood   beneath   each layer   of skin

death   is melancholic   naïve   sometimes   of beauty

people
don't   face   the dark   a bit of
                                          sadomasochism   in the psyche

admit   hidden   agenda   in fragility of   romance

I   would   rather be a   fabulous   monster

dive deep   we wear   truth in
                            a locket   how quickly
                                            we could lose   us

McQueen's Bop with the Interviewer

I've tried my best to get away
from the Little Black Dress.
That uniform makes mine eyes glaze over!
How can you trust counterfeit elegance?
There's something ignorant
in women who wear sparrows.

I want people to be afraid
of the women I dress.

Waif who needs rescuing
isn't romance.
I've seen naiveté
I know what can happen.
Someone's life is burning
from this world's brutal kiss.
I am | you are
the voyeur | the mirror.

I want people to be afraid
of the women I dress.

This is sartorial,
but, O softness.

O radiance.
Leather, locusts, shells, fur
The clothes I make
don't acquiesce.
Here teeth, and nets,
art of armor.

I want people to be afraid
of the women I dress.

Secrets & Fabulations

What do we
remember? Ironwork grate
at night, lit by a single gas lamp.

:

Tinfoil in a crow's beak,
gunshot tea brought by a stranger.

:

Lavender silk faille corset
appliqued with black lace, embroidered with jet beads.
Lapels open & plunge.

:

Collar pulled upright, tight.
Silk beaded fan a fence for the eye
& cheek to decide, *When. Now.*

:

A single brace of lilac carried
by the black casket.

:

Long skirt of patchworked denim squares,
bleach-splattered as if chainmail absorbing
soft unstill dark.

:

You stand on the step between
street & cathedral,
awareness in the heavy air.

:

What lives we have
lived. How sharp, how lush,
their shadows & textures.

Whisper the Water

White petals set loose and gathered by a single thread
Toss and toss as if it were me that flung them, not the sea.
Bed upon bed of oyster shells each turning their pearly tooth.
Judder of small hooves fling and fade,
Half moon upon half moon,
I whisper the water and you hear this
We are kin we are kin we are wind.
Whorl and whelk of gesture upon gesture
With or without that layer of your name
Across the ether we still find ourselves
The airy cage, it cannot quell.

The ear of sea inside you.
Remember how this whelming stirs you,
And drunken undulation of brazen yeses,
When the artillery of small pauses comes fully in us.
With a sum of undertones hemmed, then turned asunder
Like a thousand foundlings, unhinged from a fusillade of swells
Draw your fingers through
Maiden Hair, silvery Hart's Tongue sprung
From their silurean bed to small wings inside.
Untether your atonement, here is hushling.
Pulse here, here, feel, skirr.

Your distance is already in you.

Brushes your hunger, clean and wild.

Wind banks, begins again, here the coppery bite of salt

Sighs twist and press, each layer a simulacrum of itself.

Swells layered and purled, like waves riding through

Always more than the singular soft layers both shale and seam.

Vows carried out by the center, now all else.

Elements of sage, elements of moss, shorn, washed, thrust among

Wave and runch bestirred from cerulean shell.

The last swerve, the last anodyne,

We wander together in this swale.

Pulse here, here, feel, skirr

Untether your atonement, here is hushling.

From silurean bed to small wings inside

Maiden Hair, silvery Hart's Tongue sprung.

If you draw your fingers through

Like a thousand foundlings, unhinged from a fusillade of swells

With a sum of undertones hemmed, then turned asunder

When the artillery of small pauses comes fully in us

And drunken undulation of brazen yeses

Remember how this whelming stirs you

The ear of sea inside you.

The airy cage, it cannot quell
Across the ether we still find ourselves.
With or without that layer of your name.
Whorl and whelk of gesture upon gesture
We are kin we are kin we are wind.
I whisper the water and you hear this.
Half moon upon half moon
Judder of small hooves fling and fade
Bed upon bed of oyster shells each turning their pearly tooth
Toss and toss as if it were me that flung them, not the sea.
White petals set loose and gathered by a single thread.

We wander together in this swale,
The last swerve, the last anodyne
Wave and runch bestirred from cerulean shell.
Elements of sage, of moss, shorn and washed, thrust among
Vows carried out by the center, now all else
Always more than the singular soft layers both shale and seam.
Swells layered and purled, like waves riding through
Sighs twist and press, each layer a simulacrum of itself.
Wind banks, begins again, here the coppery bite of salt.
Brushes your hunger, clean and wild
Your distance already in you.

Dub Bill / Double Stich

Love looks not with the eyes but with the mind.
He who seeks beauty will find it. That's it, kid!

Obsession Dream

It was hope that prompted my nerve to quiver

What if the world had seen me no more   Then came

Thronging upon my recollection, he who has never

Swooned is not he who finds palaces, nor strange

Visions   They come unbidden   Colors that seemed

Faded & blurred   turn from faint to crimson

How strange & suspicious my labors must have appeared

Obsessed with shape   I worked upon my imagination

I struggled to perfect it   Mode & hour were all

That occupied me   My soul took wild interest

In trifles, passionate devotion to simple

Natural objects   Perfection has the power of thus

Affecting us   Intervals of tranquility come only

At turn of ebb & flow   All this, I saw distinctly

Charm for Protection

Here a Cocoon   spun from lambswool

Dyed with thistle   woven with wasp paper

Hood be cowled   for private thoughts

Sleeves be lined   for smell of Night

Let none harm you   Let none betray you

Wrap yourself in no Spektral affliction

Your Wound   your strength   Wild   wanted

I Dance Like Flames

McQueen Riddle (Redux)

I spin, I dip, I start fire. Wind
Can't catch my whip, my sashay
Fingertip to fall. You feel this
Lightning in me? You want
To pin me? Pass me from man to woman,
Woman to man. Egypt 2 ballroom
Floor. Kiss by kiss.
Just try to read me: I'm the one throwing
Shade, remember that. This house
Just got lucky.

I'm a Free Bitch

engineered silk   natural
    reptile, or insect   bell skirt
    once a girl, fawn   fish
   native   lightness

sea rushes quiet   dawn's fingers

moon in my blood, light changing to water
no cloak, no drapery to cover my bare legs
soon I'll long for this world and the girl
was in it

now sinuous, now rare

and yet alive like leaving

                not leaving

In this one there are dancers

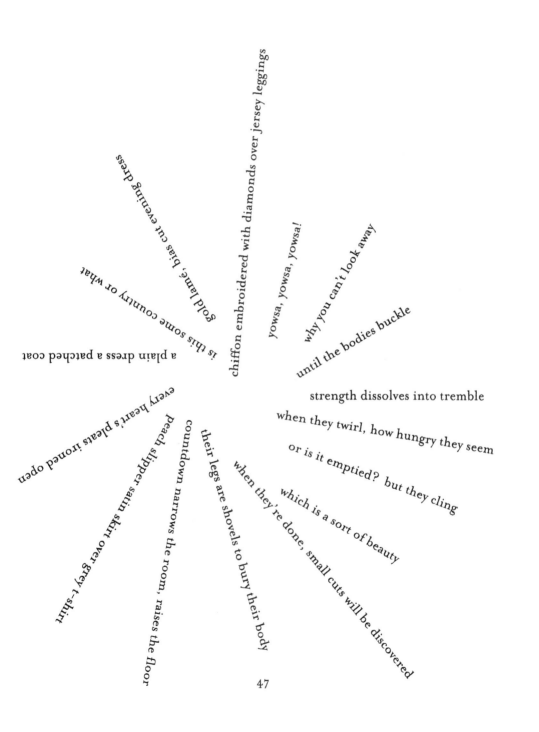

chiffon embroidered with diamonds over jersey leggings

yowsa, yowsa, yowsa!

why you can't look away

until the bodies buckle

strength dissolves into tremble

when they twirl, how hungry they seem

or is it emptied? but they cling

which is a sort of beauty

when they're done, small cuts will be discovered

their legs are shovels to bury their body

countdown narrows the room, raises the floor

peach slipper satin skirt over grey t-shirt

every heart's pleats ironed open

a plain dress a patched coat

is this some country or what

gold lamé, bias cut evening dress

Dream of Nature

In all shapes a found secret, voice of obscure wind
Organic pleasure from lines of curling mist

Nettles rot & adders sun themselves, currants
Showing deep & red on a leafless stem

While in the road I stood, a girl bore a limb
Of horns on her head & I laughed aloud

Vulgar joy, languid by its own weight,
Hues & forms allied   Rest beneath those horizontal boughs

At times the world is too much with us
My hope has been that I might fetch

Reproach from former years, whose power may spur me on
How the sea throws off the evening shade

How that which each man lived
Dies with him or is changed

McQueen Neoprene

I was   a bit of   a hooligan   wasn't I

so determined
to drum into   my life   in   my persona

people   wasn't given   me   no leeway

I forgot what   I was   born to do

it was   to answer   myself   to accept

I was doing   a job   mischief
     I didn't want   all my
     demons

which was   conflict, angst   but the last years

have been good

my work   I've   made   a conscious
                                             effort   I want to
                                                                     communicate
stillness now   like that of
                         music
                         or sex, after: resting
                         what they call
                                sadness
                                        though   it is not
                                                            sadness

[I knew a woman when I saw one, though]

I knew a woman when I saw one, though
not, as they say, in the usual way [laughs]. I saw
the skeleton beneath, opened my eyes,
which had seen only my thoughts,

and thought the sky good to eat. I became
methodical as nature. These selves of which we
build ourselves up—noble, humane, greedy,
vicious - too many for nothing. I had

the look of innocence, though technically
that word no longer applied [laughs again]. I embroidered
orchards, made damask bloom and fade,
more auroral than the white sun as it sank,

so that s/he could breathe, *I am alive.* Each
time, an evening we made so astonishing.

McQueen Cashmere

remind me when you can't take any more

war disaster work pain fashion

and still your thought should have

love is the lesson to be learnt

both answer and question you are more than costume

inside you find at last your own creations

House of McQueen

Blush slash shocks callous London. Worth
built his own house.
Others consider cloth's ripple, want
a red flare to flaunt.

Finery's patterns indeed shift to threads, line
draws down interred silhouette.
But while we live awhile here
pattern and line gather

quiet that is anything
but quiet. Each time, dream delights
as if a small wing beats, and leaves
dance under our transient skins.

Winged

The old masters
got them wrong,

their locations,
at least. Not pinned

at the spine like a moth's
or the bone blade spurt.

From the tiny bloom
of sternum I swept

over shoulders, fanned,
arc'd. Slit for heavy arms.

*How on earth do you
expect to walk in them?* Ha.

Be/hold balsa ribbons
planed, laced, bindings,

not for flight but descent.
How will you care for me,

keep me from fire.
It sings, you know,

Consecration.
Consolation,

a promise to be ever
sewn into the sun.

Silhouette for the 21ˢᵗ Century

The naked sound of the body sounds
Like a trumpet. I announce a new world
In which your madness and my madness
At the point of a needle, is my love, spinning.

Drop a hard landscape of bone & shadow.
I am in love with birds. Oh! Sprinkled
With a little gold-leaf. What is real
I suppose, will endure. Shape that moves

Forwards & backwards. Utter logic of form
& color, something in God-language, in
Spite of all this unfathomable language.
I gave you my imaginary hand & you gave

me your imaginary hand & we walk together
In imaginary land over the earthly ground.

Autobiography of Alexander McQueen

I'm a romantic, really—
I try to protect people.
People say I do it for the shock value
I just like exploring the sinister side of life.

I try to protect people.
We all get ugly in the end, don't we?
I explore the sinister side of life—
I can't keep rehashing the good, the bad, the ugly.

We all get ugly in the end, don't we.
I sound like I'm contradicting myself but that's me all over!
You can't keep rehashing the same concepts.
I'm trying to weave a new fabric, but the loom doesn't exist.

I sound like I'm contradicting myself, but
I grew up with a lot of ignorance; it showed me a bigger picture.
I'm trying to weave a new fabric which doesn't exist
All about Lee the Cockney.

I grew up with a lot of racism and homophobia, so I feel
You really don't need a beautiful face.
It was all about Lee the Cockney oik,
But now it's about the Company, and peace of mind.

Fashion should predict the time we're in.
You need proportion, color, cut and style.
It's about the company you keep, and peace of mind.
I really don't think you need a beautiful face.

You need proportion, color, cut, and style,
Solitude, and a blank canvas to work from.
Fashion should predict the time we're in, not reflect it.
Life is a transformation!

Solitude is the blank canvas I work from.
Life is a transformation.
People will say I did it for the shock value—
But I'm just a romantic, really.

But There on the Shining

parking garage lit with candles
encloses room of white wilderness

then out of

[wolf howl   sutures]   *air*

coyote fur peeks from inside a sleeve
& between shoulder seams

black fantail birdcut jackets

we watch | each other | in isolation | sharp-edged moonlight

How   It is
sumptuous roses painted into tan leather   shift

frosty pink roped & cabled   sweater

grey quilted   shrug   comfort

to handle a life with care, even if care
was not what was wanted

aluminum coiled corset | Ndebe | Cossak | worn like a shield

the mass and majesty of this world, all

          that carries weight

             and always weighs the same

a man chucking more and more snow into the wind machine while
another shouts, More, more! I want this to be like a snow-shaker!

bodice of rock crystal
light inside it

these girls don't *look over his shoulder*

metallic skirt etched with gothic scrolls
reflects intricate light

white rabbit coat voluptuous as snow fox underbelly

laser-cut snowflake ivory silk | skirt over tulle underskirt | lets the light

snow like
flowers

---------------------- 13 skaters
                                        quick quick to music------------

61

midnight   stars

                                        and   you

Joyce & Lee

If any era, which one would it be? *15th century Flemish*

Who are your favourite artists? *I think composers*

What do your Scottish roots mean to you? *Everything*

What is your most terrifying fear? *Dying before you*

What was it about her presence that captivated you? *She started laughing*

What makes your heart miss a beat? *Love.*

Lee

I.

I feel
deep
anarchy
the calm
part
getting into it
captures
dying before
your heart
misses
a
beat

2.

I would

have liked

the past

the sympathetic way

they approached

solitude

whatever I

believe

history

follows

where I

come

in

3.

World a blank
canvas What home
I have come
from my roots
the deep sea
fantastic
other times
the streets
Whenever lost
I go straight into
the past Ask
the next one
[laughs]

Notes

The epigraphs are from, respectively:

    Leaves of Hypnos, Grossman; 1st Edition (1973) by Rene Char

    (Author), Cid Corman (Translator)

    Interview with Sarah Burton by Jess McCartner-Morley,

    "Alexander McQueen: into the light," *The Guardian* — February 10,

    2015.

"[When the body becomes everything it is given]" is after the
McQueen collection *Highland Rape*, autumn/winter 1995–96.

"Bumsters" is after McQueen's infamous "bumsters"trousers,
premiered at his collection *Taxi Driver* autumn/winter 1993-94.

The title *"Let's make a dress from these"* is a quote attributed to McQueen
as he walked into his workroom with a handful of red medical
slides; the poem is after the subsequent dress, from the McQueen
collection *Voss*, spring/summer 2001.

In "McQueen Linen", the first line is a quote from Alexander
McQueen. The poem contains an adaptation of a line by Mark
Doty in his poem "Bill's Story" in *My Alexandria*, University of Illinois
Press, 1993, *"If you take everything, you've got to let everything go."* The skull is
a motif employed by McQueen.

"& for a moment they" is after a dress from the McQueen collection *Sarabande*, spring/summer 2007.

"I like a good Grimm tale" is a quote attributed to McQueen; the poem is after an ensemble from the McQueen collection *Supercalifragilisticexpialidocious*, autumn/winter 2002-03.

"McQueen Self-Portrait as Bestiary" was inspired in form by the poem "A Bestiary" by Spencer Reece in *The Clerk's Tale*, Houghton Mifflin. 2004.

"Savile Row, 1985" contains verified and unverified biographical details. That he wrote a slur in the interlining of a coat for the Prince of Wales while an apprentice may likely be a rumor started by Alexander McQueen, unverified by the firm he had apprenticed with, who subsequently recalled the coats, took them apart, and reported that they found nothing.

In "Bespoke," each respective stanza is made from vocabularies of seven women who were muses / patrons / friends of Alexander McQueen. I gathered these words from print and video interviews, presentations, tweets, and press releases; the arrangement and intentions are my own. Also, the first of these is after Lucie Brock-Broido.

"From the Shoulder" is after a jacket from the McQueen collection *It's a jungle out there!*, autumn/winter 1997-98.

The acrostic in "Haute Couture" is a quote from Alexander McQueen ("...at the end of the day, they're only clothes"). This poem was influenced by the interview Alexander McQueen gave Nick Knight in 2010, *SHOWstudio: Alexander McQueen, S/S 2010 RTW, Plato's Atlantis Interview.* http://showstudio.com/project/platos_atlantis/interview

In "McQueen Tartan", the first line is a quote from Alexander McQueen. "I would rather be a fabulous monster" is a quote from Alexander Woollcott.

"Secrets & Fabulations" is after an ensemble from the McQueen collection *Dante*, autumn/winter 1996-1997.

"Whisper the Water" is after the "Oyster Dress" from the McQueen collection *Irere*, spring/summer 2003.

"Charm for Protection" is after a coat from the McQueen collection *In Memory of Elizabeth Howe, 1692*, fall/winter 2007.

The answer to the riddle in "I Dance Like Flames: McQueen Riddle (Redux)" is *La Dame Bleu*, the name of McQueen's spring/summer 2008 collection in honor of his friend Isabella Blow. This para-translation is based on the translation of the Anglo-

Saxon "Riddle 30: I Dance like Flames" (answer: A willow tree) by David Constantine, "The Word Exchange: Anglo-Saxon Poems in Translation", copyright 2011 Eds. Grey Delanty and Michael Matto. Norton.

"I'm a Free Bitch" is after a dress from the McQueen collection *Plato's Atlantis* spring/summer 2010 and takes its title from a portion of a line in the song "Bad Romance" by Lady Gaga, which premiered at this show.

"In this one there are dancers" is after *Deliverance*, McQueen's spring/summer 2005 collection inspired by the film *They Shoot Horses, Don't They?*, which was based on the dance marathons of the 1930s.

In "McQueen Neoprene" the last line is from Carl Phillips's poem "Late Apollo", *The Rest of Love*, Farrar, Straus and Giroux, 2004. Some of the lines left to right are quotes from McQueen.

In "McQueen Cashmere" the line "love is the lesson to be learnt" is from Linton Kwesi Johnson's poem "Seasons of the Heart," *Mi Revalueshanary Fren*, Copper Canyon Press, 2006.

"House of McQueen" is written with the pattern of "At Briggflatts Meeting House" by Basil Bunting, in *Complete Poems*, New Directions Books copyright 2003. Charles Worth (1835-1895) was the first designer to own his own fashion house and is widely thought of as the father of haute couture.

"Winged" is after a corset from the McQueen collection *No. 13*, spring/summer 1999.

"From the Autobiography of Alexander McQueen" is composed of quotes pulled from print and video interviews with Lee Alexander McQueen.

"But There on the Shining" is after the McQueen collection *The Overlook* autumn/winter 1999 and takes its title and italicized lines from W.H. Auden's "The Shield of Achilles". The last line is a reference to "Midnight, Stars, and You" by Ray Noble, sung by Al Bowlly, which played at the end of McQueen's show *The Overlook,* and Stanley Kubric film *The Shining*.

The poems in "Joyce & Lee" and "Lee" are erasures from "Meeting the Queen was Like Falling in Love", *The Guardian*, April 20, 2004, in which Joyce McQueen interviews her son.

I made the following out of text I found (and occasionally corrupted) from these respective sources:

"Shears"—*Complete Poems* by Basil Bunting. New Directions Books, copyright 2003.

"Needles"—*The Selected Poems of Frank O'Hara by Frank O'Hara*, edited by Donald Allen, first published in Great Britain by Carcanet Press Ltd, copyright 1991 by Maureen Granville-Smith.

"Fabrication"—*Visible Shivers and Four Door Guide* by Tom Raworth.

"Small seams"—*New Selected Poems and Translations* by Ezra Pound, Ed. Richard Sieburth. New Directions Press, 2010 and *Early Writings: Poems and Prose* by Ezra Pound. Penguin Books, 2005.

"Studded"—*Selected Poems* by James Schuyler. Farrar, Straus and Giroux, 1988.

"Dub Bill / Double Stich"—*A Midsummer's Night Dream* by William Shakespeare ("Love looks not with the eyes but with the mind" was tattooed on McQueen's right upper arm); phrases spoken by the fashion and street photographer Bill Cunningham, as evidenced in *Bill Cunningham New York* (2010 documentary, Zeitgeist Films).

"Dream of Nature"— *Collected Poems* by William Wordsworth, Penguin. Ed Nicolas.

"Obsession Dream"—*The Pit and the Pendulum* by Edgar Allen Poe.

"[I knew a woman when I saw one, though]"—*Orlando* by Virginia Woolf.

"Silhouette for the 21st Century"—*The Collected Books of Jack Spicer* by Jack Spicer, edited by Robin Blaser, Black Sparrow Books 1975.

The following books and other sources helped me to write this one:

Alexander McQueen: Savage Beauty catalog to the exhibit organized by The Costume Institute, The Metropolitan Museum of Art in 2011, by Andrew Bolton, curator, with contributions by Susannah Frankel and Tim Blanks; Photography by Sølve Sundsbø

Exhibit of Alexander McQueen: Savage Beauty at the Victoria & Albert Museum in London (2015) curated by Claire Wilcox

Alexander McQueen: Evolution by Katherine Gleason

Extreme Beauty: The Body Transformed by Harold Koda

Gods and Kings: The Rise and Fall of Alexander McQueen and John Galliano by Dana Thomas

Alexander McQueen: The Life and the Legacy by Judith Watt, Daphne Guinness (Foreword)

Love Looks Not with the Eyes: Thirteen Years with Lee Alexander McQueen by Anne Deniau

McDowell's Directory of Twentieth Century Fashion by Colin McDowell

Savile Row Bespoke Tailoring Terms
http://www.savilerowbespoke.com/about-us/tailoring-terms/

Acknowledgements

I am deeply grateful to the editors of these journals for publishing many of the poems in this collection, though some were subsequently slightly altered:

Found Poetry Review, Ilanot, JMWW, Kettle Blue Review, Pool, Ricochet Review, Rogue Agent, Rust + Moth, TINGE, Tinderbox Poetry Journal, Tupelo Quarterly, and *Watershed Review.*

My deepest gratitude to Vievee Francis.

Many thanks to the City of Chicago Department of Cultural Affairs and Special Events, Illinois Arts Council, Kimmel-Harding Nelson Center for the Arts, Midwest Writing Center and Sisters of St. Benedict at Benet House Retreat Center at St. Mary Monastery, Ragdale Foundation, the Vermont Studio Center, Tamara Adams of Emandal, and Barbara Barnard and Jim Barnard, without whose support of quiet, meadows, rivers, and libraries, this book would not have happened.

Thank you to my earliest teachers who encouraged me when I was at Bethany College in Kansas, including Linda Lewis and Carolyn Kahler, and to Mitch "Mitar" Covic when I was a student at Urban Life/Chicago Center, to Catherine Bowman and Liz Rosenburg who taught me at the Fine Arts Work Center, to Marie Howe who taught me at the Southhampton Writers Workshop, the Community of Writers at Squaw Valley, including my "Jeffery House" cohort, and to my teachers at the School of the Art Institute of Chicago, especially Calvin Forbes and Elise Paschen. Thank you to Sterling Plumpp for opening the door.

To my alive-to-the work readers Virginia Bell, Ralph Hamilton, Rob Moore, Kevin Simmonds, Candace Vogler, Hank Vogler, and Andrea Witzke-Slot: A million thank yous. This book is better for your input. Thank you as well to Peter O'Leary and my classmates in his University of Chicago course, who gave me invaluable feedback on several of these poems in their earliest forms.

For their support of this book, I thank Maureen Alsop, Tiff Beatty, Jan Bottiglieri, Dolores Cross, Robert Devendorf, Carol Eding, Chris Green, David Jones, Beth McDermott, Kelly Morgan, and to ZoeAnne Nepolello, Intern Extraordinaire.

Thank you to the *RHINO* community of poets, workshop leaders, and especially editors, with whom I spent many Thursday evenings discussing, arguing, and learning about poetry in ways I think of as a master class. Thank you to Martha Vertreace-Doody, whose *RHINO* workshop gave me the idea to write a lot of poems about someone very different than me.

To Martha Rhodes, Mari Coates, Clairissa Long, James Fujinami Moore, Ryan Murphy, and all the people at Four Way Books, thank you for your beautiful work.

Thank you to my parents, and to my grandmother, Frances Caroline Smith. To all my families, thank you for your support. To my Love, Marc Monaghan—this book is for you.

To Lee Alexander McQueen, wherever you are. Thank you for your presence, gifts, purpose, and all of the dark and light you shared with the world.

Publication of this book was made possible by grants and donations. We are also grateful to those individuals who participated in our 2017 Build a Book Program. They are:

Anonymous (6), Evan Archer, Sally Ball, Jan Bender-Zanoni, Zeke Berman, Kristina Bicher, Laurel Blossom, Carol Blum, Betsy Bonner, Mary Brancaccio, Lee Briccetti, Deirdre Brill, Anthony Cappo, Carla & Steven Carlson, Caroline Carlson, Stephanie Chang, Tina Chang, Liza Charlesworth, Maxwell Dana, Machi Davis, Marjorie Deninger, Lukas Fauset, Monica Ferrell, Emily Flitter, Jennifer Franklin, Martha Webster & Robert Fuentes, Chuck Gillett, Dorothy Goldman, Dr. Lauri Grossman, Naomi Guttman & Jonathan Mead, Steven Haas, Mary Heilner, Hermann Hesse, Deming Holleran, Nathaniel Hutner, Janet Jackson, Christopher Kempf, David Lee, Jen Levitt, Howard Levy, Owen Lewis, Paul Lisicky, Sara London & Dean Albarelli, David Long, Katie Longofono, Cynthia Lowen, Ralph & Mary Ann Lowen, Donna Masini, Louise Mathias, Catherine McArthur, Nathan McClain, Gregory McDonald, Britt Melewski, Kamilah Moon, Carolyn Murdoch, Rebecca & Daniel Okrent, Tracey Orick, Zachary Pace, Gregory Pardlo, Allyson Paty, Marcia & Chris Pelletiere, Taylor Pitts, Eileen Pollack, Barbara Preminger, Kevin Prufer, Vinode Ramgopal, Martha Rhodes, Peter & Jill Schireson, Roni & Richard Schotter, Soraya Shalforoosh, Peggy Shinner, James Snyder & Krista Fragos, Megan Staffel, Alice St. Claire-Long, Robin Taylor, Marjorie & Lew Tesser, Boris Thomas, Judith Thurman, Susan Walton, Calvin Wei, Abby Wender, Bill Wenthe, Allison Benis White, Elizabeth Whittlesey, Hao Wu, Monica Youn, and Leah Zander.